Hooray for Holyrood

political cartoons
by Frank Boyle

Argyll
publishing

First published 2002
Argyll Publishing
Glendaruel
Argyll PA22 3AE
Scotland
www.skoobe.biz

The author has asserted his moral rights.

**British Library Cataloguing-in-Publication Data.
A catalogue record for this book is available
from the British Library.**

ISBN 1 902831 50 0

Origination Cordfall Ltd, Glasgow

Printing Bell & Bain Ltd, Glasgow

To my parents

Contents

Foreword	5
Scotland	7
United Kingdom	41
Foreign Affairs	67
Edinburgh	81
Sport	107

Foreword

This book is a selection of my work in the Edinburgh Evening News since March 1999. This neatly covers the historic first term of the new Scottish Parliament, which has provided me with lots of cartoon material. Hence the title Hooray for Holyrood.

Political cartoons tend by their nature to knock politicians but I wanted the overall message to be positive. Like the majority of Scots I voted for the parliament and I would like to see it succeed. However, the book is not just about Holyrood. It covers subjects as diverse as the campaign to save the Morningside toilets to global warming.

Most politicians are quite thick-skinned and seem to enjoy being the subject of cartoons no matter how scurrilous. One exception was the fundementalist US preacher Pat Robertson. He threatened to sue me over a cartoon I did of him (see page 12). This was in my first week at the paper. In the end he backed down. So in the spirit of open comment on the doings of those in power, if there are any who were offended the first time, they have the opportunity with this book to be offended all over again. For the rest, enjoy the book.

There are several people without whose support the book would not have happened. I would like to thank John McLellan, editor of the Evening News who gave me the job. Ian Stewart, the current editor, has also been very supportive. Thanks are due to the staff of the paper, especially the political editor Ian Swanson and Alison Templeton. I would like to thank Donald Ross of The Scotsman whose advice is always wise, and Shaun McLaren who gave great help with the cover design.

Among other readers, I would like to acknowledge the continued support and encouragement of the late Isabella Morrison of Linlithgow whose frequent emails were a great source of strength. She would have been delighted to see this collection as a book.

Having spent two years looking for a publisher, Derek Rodger of Argyll deserves a big thanks for saying yes, when others had said no.

Frank Boyle
September 2002

Scotland

August 6th, 2001

The cost of the new parliament building continue to rise and red light tolerance zones are in the news.

February 3rd, 2000
The cost of the new parliament, designed by Spanish architect Enric Miralles, keeps rising and Scottish Opera is bailed out again by the Executive.

December 21, 2001
Big demand for Lego Hogwarts Castle and new parliament building . . . still costing more.

June 1, 1999
Burns's 'A Man's a Man' to be sung at Parliament opening.
Lyrics might be too left-wing for today's New Labour.

March 19, 1999
Anti-gay US preacher Pat Robertson did a deal with the Bank of Scotland.
Huge protests caused the bank to withdraw.

November 29, 2001
New First Minister Jack McConnell sacks most of the previous Cabinet.

April, 1999

Scotland play France at rugby in Paris during the election campaign.

September 21, 1999
The video of the opening ceremony of the new Scottish Parliament is released.

June 6, 2001
Lacklustre SNP Convenor John Swinney needs Sean Connery's support during the General Election campaign.

May 6th 1999
Election day dawns for for the new Scottish Parliament.

March 31, 2000

As part of the UK government's dispersal programme asylum seekers arrive in Glasgow.

December 1, 1999
Royal Bank vs Bank of Scotland takeover battle.
Recent riots at the G7 summit in Seattle against the effects of global capitalism.

November 14, 2001
Jack McConnell takes over as leading candidate for Labour leadership
and election as First Minister. The Northern Alliance enter Kabul after the fall of the Taliban.

July 19, 2000
The chief of clan Macleod threatens to sell the Cuillin mountains.

February 7, 2002
Conservative leader David McLetchie admits he was once a Mason.

January 21, 2000
The shambolic launch of Stagecoach managing director Brian Soutar's campaign against the abolition of Section 28. Expected celebrities failed to turn up.

November 26, 1999
South Park movie out. SNP MSP Kenny McAskill is arrested at England v Scotland game.

May 26, 2000
Marks & Spencer cancel their contract with Daks Simpson
in West Lothian making many workers redundant.

April 4, 2001
First Minister Henry McLeish puts his foot in it by dismissing the foot and mouth epidemic as 'a little problem' on a visit to US. (For some reason Henry 'the Fonz' Winkler was there.)

April 4, 2002
It emerges that the new parliament building has not been wind tested;
MSPs vote for a salary increase.

April, 1999
SNP supporter Sean Connery comes under pressure, living in tax exile in the Bahamas.

December 4, 2000
Sean Connery is banned from giving money to the SNP.

June 21, 2002
Lothian police are accused of faking crime figures.
A bitter SNP candidate selection process is ongoing.

January 25, 2001
Scottish Executive disagree over free care for the elderly.
The true site of the Battle of Bannockburn is discovered.

December 6, 2000
Overcrowding on Scotrail trains.

October, 2001
Mosques are attacked in the aftermath of September 11.

August 17, 2002
Lord James Douglas Hamilton proposed that Princes Street Gardens West
be renamed as a memorial to the late Queen Mother.

April 11, 2001
Motorola close their Bathgate plant.

April 11, 2001
Executive announce an extension to the M74
and pensioners are to receive free bus passes in two years time.

April 11, 2001
News leaks out that Scottish Secretary Helen Liddell has been strategically kept
in the background during the General Election campaign.

March 21, 2001
After the Scottish Qualifications Authority exam result fiasco the previous year,
Education Minister Sam Galbraith comes under increasing pressure.

August 26, 2002
EU threaten to ban th e use of sheep's stomachs in haggis.

June, 2002
Plans to use Scots language signs for the new Parliament building are rejected.
MSP Margo MacDonald is effectively deselected as an SNP candidate.

United Kingdom

August 11, 1999

Prince Phillip, in another gaffe while visiting a Racal factory, says a faulty fusebox must have been put in by an Indian. Racal make brake systems for trains.

June 21, 2001
New Labour refuse to implement election promise to ban smoking adverts.

October 10, 2000
Long term effects of Ecstasy can be drastic say doctors. Chaos on the privatised railways.

June 28, 2001
New Labour appears keen to distance itself from the Trade Unions and suck up to big business.

November 23, 1999
Former Tory Party Chairman and author Lord Archer is jailed.
A new James Bond movie is on general release.

September 5, 2001
Pupils at Holy Cross school in Belfast are harassed by Loyalist protestors.

August 1, 2001
The government wants to sell off the London Underground despite the Railtrack fiasco.
'Only Fools and Horses' returns to tv screens.

September 25, 2001
Prince William enrols at posh St Andrews University.

March 27, 2000
Ulster Unionist leader David Trimble is under pressure from his traditionalist members.

September 11, 2001
NHS privatisation.

June 19, 2000
England fans riot at Euro Championships.
The Tories are very anti-Europe.

Cash-starved air traffic control to be privatised.

October 6, 2000
The last Mini rolls off the production line.
Ann Widdecombe demands a hard line on cannabis users.

October 26, 2000
Hatfield rail crash.

March 25, 2002
Prime Minister Tony Blair is accused of becoming a clone of Margaret Thatcher.

November 21, 2000
Royal Mail stops using Postman Pat for promotion.
Lots of strikes in sorting offices.

May 4, 2001
Great Train robber Ronnie Biggs back in Britain.

May 23, 2001
The film 'Pearl Harbour' opens.
The Tories trail badly in the polls.

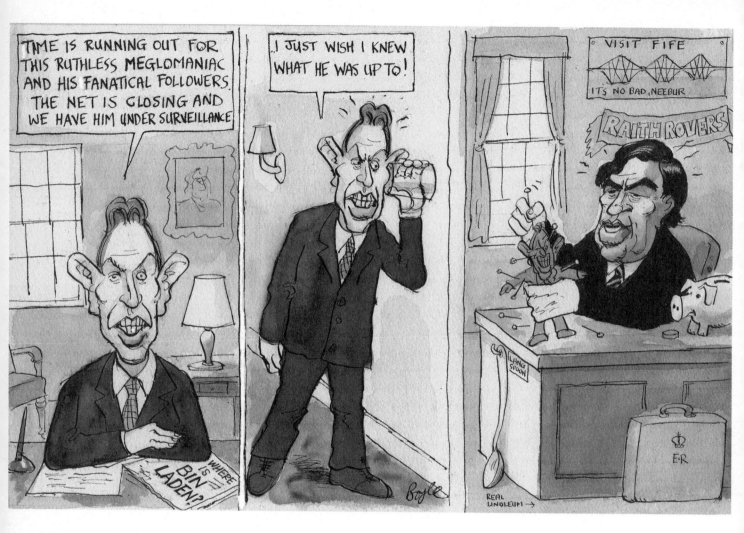

November 20, 2001
Hunt for Bin Laden goes on.
Brown v Blair power struggle in the headlines.

December 13, 2001
Consignia in trouble – thousands face the chop.

December 14, 1999
John Prescott demoted from Transport Minister.
Lord McDonald takes over.

July 6, 2000
Water cannon used to disperse demonstrating Orangemen at Drumcree.

October 2, 2000

The film 'Billy Elliot' opens as William Hague claims to have drunk fourteen pints a day.

October 19, 1999
Ulster Unionist leader David Trimble says Orange Walks
could be seen as tourist attractions in Northern Ireland.

May 1, 2000
Official Labour Party candidate Frank Dobson heads for defeat
against Ken Livingstone in the London Mayor election.

Foreign Affairs

May 18, 2001

President George W Bush wants to open up Alaska to oil exploration.

July 4, 2001
Oil man George W Bush ignores global warming threat.

CHILEAN WITH A BAD BACK
2000

Hospital

CHILEANS WITH BAD BACKS
1973

Boyle

January 7, 2000
Former Chilean dictator General Pinochet, leader of the bloody coup in 1973,
is still under house arrest in London and claims to have a bad back.

July 26, 2001
The government announce a get-tough policy on loan sharks.

July 25, 2001
Chinese flag stolen from outside Consulate in Edinburgh.

August 23, 2001

Calls are made to boycott the Perrier Award for comedy acts. Perrier own Nestlé who market dried milk to third world countries with dire consequences.

September 6, 1999
Many are massacred by Indonesian troops during the election in East Timor.

March 15, 2002
President Bush criticises Robert Mugabe's election in Zimbabwe.

Lady Thatcher backs former Chilean dictator General Pinochet
when he is placed under house arrest while on a visit to London.

OH, LITTLE TOWN OF BETHLEHEM
HOW STILL WE SEE THEE LIE......

October 24, 2001
Israeli forces move into Bethlehem.

September 12, 2001

April 5, 2002
McDonald's win the 'Keep Edinburgh Tidy' award despite their environmental record.

November 27, 2000
President Bush reneges on the Kyoto agreement.
With 4% of the world's population, the US produces 25% of its pollution.

Edinburgh

September 9, 1999
Morningside residents campaign against a Superloo.

July 5, 2000
MSP Tommy Sheridan proposes cannabis cafés in Scotland.

February 8, 2002
Pupils at Tony Blair's old school Fettes College are caught smoking cannabis.

November 27, 2000
A blanket shortage at Edinburgh Royal Infirmary.

September 9, 2000
Edinburgh Council refuse to allow any more sex shops.

January 10, 2002
Reports of rubbish dumping in the newly reopened Union Canal.

August 24, 2000
Former Leith MP Ron Brown may become Libyan Consul.

June 15, 2000
Anarchist protestors threaten to dig up streets.
The Council's plan for Galleries shopping centre under Princes Street is scrapped.

August 28, 2001

Church allows British Telecom to put a mobile phone mast in their tower, despite protests from locals.

February 6, 2001
The continuing saga of a transport link to Edinburgh airport.

June 1, 2000

Because of yuppification, the traditional Leith pageant fails to attract much interest. It may close down.

February 19, 2002
The Women's Royal Voluntary Service is replaced by Starbucks
as providers of refreshments at the new Edinburgh Royal Infirmary.

February 2, 2000

Plans are announced for a major redevelopment at Granton including a marina.

June 10, 1999
An assistant at the fish counter in Safeway's Morningside is caught selling cannabis.

June 2, 2000
Zen Buddhist classes begin at Saughton prison.

October 23, 2001
Another guided bus scheme is announced to replace the ill-fated CERT.

January 24, 2000
Prince William may join the 'Yahs' at Edinburgh University.

March 1, 2000
Grampian Foods close their Newbridge factory making the workforce redundant.

May 16, 2000
An Edinburgh church holds services in a pub and offers a free pint to those who join in.

March 25, 1999
Church of Scotland urges ministers to make services more lively.

April 26, 2000
Transport Minister Sarah Boyack approves Midlothian Council plan for new A701 despite local opposition.

February 5, 2002
Prisoners may be allowed home for the weekend.

August 6, 1999
Complaints about too many Festival street performers in Edinburgh's High Street.

May 24, 2002
Lord Provost Eric Milligan has £700 worth of dental treatment to whiten teeth.
The Queen holds a Golden Jubilee garden party at Holyrood.

December 5, 2001
The capital's property prices go through the roof.

Sport

December 5, 2000
Lord Provost Eric Milligan met the Pope in Rome. Hearts were doing badly.

November 6, 2001
The hunt for Osama Bin Laden is stepped up.
Hearts fans demonstrate against chairman Chris Robinson after a string of bad results.

April 20, 2001
Former Hearts owner Wallace Mercer, the man who tried to shut down Hibs,
returns to Edinburgh after years in the South of France.

February 4, 2000
Scotland play Italy at rugby in Rome . . . and lose.

May 11, 2000
Hibs dig up their turf at Easter Road and sell it to fans.

October 11, 1999
Despite now having our own parliament and 'a new sense of maturity',
most Scots support the New Zealand All Blacks against England.

April 16, 2001
Easter Weekend: Hibs reach Scottish Cup Final;
Bishop Holloway says Tommy Sheridan is a Christ-like figure.

November 10, 1999
Scandal of free tickets for Scotland v England – many organisations involved in the scam.

October 25, 2000

Hearts beleaguered chairman Chris Robinson is criticised for selling off the club's best assets.
At the same time Ingleston market is raided by police in search of counterfeit goods.

May 22, 2002
A grass roof for the proposed new Council HQ.

January 18, 2000
Hibs tour Trinidad & Tobago.

April 28, 2000
Murrayfield stadium flooded days before the Rugby League Cup Final.

October 18, 1999
Only those with English accents could telephone
their purchase of tickets for England v Scotland at Wembley.

August 8, 2001
Scotland campaigns for the Ryder Cup; the Holyrood building project labours under more bad publicity.

August 22, 2000

Tom Farmer claimed Edinburgh Council were anti-Hibs after turning down
planning permission for a stand at their Easter Road stadium.

April 15, 1999
Edinburgh Council gets tough on antisocial neighbours. Hibs win promotion; Hearts are struggling.

May 26, 2002
SNP's Andrew Wilson says Scots should show a greater maturity
and self-confidence and support England in the World Cup.

October 23, 2000
Henry McLeish is elected First Minister. Hibs, managed by namesake Alex, beat Hearts 6–2.

April 29, 2002

Livingston FC qualify for Europe. Right wing anti-immigrant Jean Marie Le Pen does well in first round of French presidential election.

Visit Frank Boyle's website
www.boylecartoon.co.uk
email: info@boylecartoon.co.uk